NEW 영어교과서 따라쓰기

기획 : Y&M 어학연구소

와이 앤 엠

차 례

NEW 영어교과서 따라쓰기

1. 인사

 단어를 배워 봅시다.

<u>hello</u>

<u>fine</u>

<u>goodbye</u>

 문장을 배워 봅시다.

Hello.

Hello, Nancy.

단어를 따라 써봅시다.

hello
안녕 · 헬로우

hello

hello

hello

fine
좋은 · 퐈인

fine

fine

fine

goodbye
안녕 · 굿바이

goodbye

goodbye

goodbye

문장을 따라 써봅시다.

Hello.   Hello.

Hello, Nancy.   Hello, Nancy.

단어를 배워 봅시다.

thank

morning

sorry

 문장을 배워 봅시다.

⭐ 단어를 따라 써봅시다.

thank
감사하다 · 쌩크

thank

thank

thank

morning
아침인사 · 모닝

morning

morning

morning

sorry
미안 · 쏘리

sorry

sorry

sorry

⭐ 문장을 따라 써봅시다.

Goodbye, Nancy.   Goodbye, Nancy.

Goodbye, Tom.   Goodbye, Tom.

Hi, Tom.

안녕, 톰.

Thank you, Nancy.

고마워, 낸시.

Goodbye Song Won.

잘 있어, 성원.

문장을 따라 써 봅시다.

Hi, Tom.

Hi, Tom.   Hi, Tom.

Thank you, Nancy.

Thank you, Nancy.

Goodbye, Song Won.

Goodbye, Song Won.

인사

Hello
안녕

[helóu 헬로우]

hello hello hello

fine
훌륭한

[fain 퐈인]

fine fine fine fine fine

Goodbye
안녕(작별인사)

[gudbai 굿바이]

goodbye goodbye goodbye

thank
감사하다

[θæŋk 쌩크]

thank thank thank

morning
아침인사

[mɔ́ːrniŋ
모-ㄹ닝]

morning morning morning

sorry
미안하다

[sɔ́ːri 써-뤼]

sorry   sorry   sorry   sorry

glad
기쁜

[glæd 기쁜, 반가운]

glad   glad   glad   glad

name
이름

[neim 이름]

name   name   name

age
나이

[ediʒ 에이쥐]

age   age   age   age   age

welcome
환영하다

[wélkəm 웰컴]

welcome   welcome   welcome

excuse
용서하다

[ikskjúːz 익스큐즈]

excuse   excuse   excuse

1. 다음 단어의 뜻이 서로 맞은 것끼리 선으로 연결하고 따라 써 봅시다.

❶ hello

• 잘있어

h _____

❷ goodbye

• 고마워

g _____

❸ thank

• 너

t _____

❹ you

• 안녕

y _____

2. 앞에서 배운 단어를 아래에 한 번 더 따라 써봅시다.

hello

hello

goodbye

goodbye

thank

thank

you

you

3. 보기에서 알맞은 단어를 찾아 문장을 완성하고, 아래에 따라 써 봅시다.

| 보기 | Nancy | Sung-Won | you |

❶ hello _____ . 안녕, 성원

❷ goodbye _____ . 잘있어, 낸시

❸ thank _____ . 고마워(상대에게).

❹ goodbye _____ . 잘있어, 성원아.

4. 앞에서 배운 단어를 아래에 따라 써봅시다.

hello   Sung-Won.

goodbye   Nancy.

thank   you.

goodbye   Sung-Won.

2. 탈것들

 단어를 배워 봅시다.

a car

a taxi

a ship

 문장을 배워 봅시다.

This is a car.

That is a ship.

car

자동차 · 카

car

car

taxi

택시 · 택시

taxi

taxi

ship

배 · 쉽

ship

ship

★ 문장을 따라 써봅시다.

This is a car.　　This is a car.

That is a taxi.　　That is a taxi.

This is a ship.　　That is a ship.

단어를 배워봅시다.

a bus

an airplane

an ambulance

 문장을 배워봅시다.

This is a bus.

That is an airplane.

20

단어를 따라 써봅시다.

bus

버스 · **버스**

bus

bus

airplane

비행기 에어플레인

airplane

airplane

ambulance

구급차 엠뷰런스

ambulance

ambulance

문장을 따라 써봅시다.

This is a bus.　　This is a bus.

That is an airplane.

That is an ambulance

This is a taxi.
이것은 택시이다.

That is an ambulance.
저것은 구급차이다.

That is a train.
저것은 기차이다.

22

문장을 따라 써봅시다.

This is a taxi.

This is a taxi.   This is a taxi.

This is a taxi.   This is a taxi.

That is an ambulance.

That is an ambulance.

That is an ambulance.

That is a train.

That is a train.   That is a train.

That is a train.   That is a train.

탈것들

airplane
비행기
[ɛərplén
에얼플레인]

airplane   airplane   airplane

ambulance
구급차
[æmbjələns
앰뷸런스]

ambulance   ambulance

bicycle
자전거
[báisikəl바이시클]

bicycle   bicycle   bicycle

boat
보트, 작은배
[bout 보웃트]

boat   boat   boat   boat

bus
버스
[bʌs 버스]

bus   bus   bus   bus

car
자동차

[kɑːr 카-ㄹ]

car   car   car   car   car

ship
배

[ʃip 쉽]

ship   ship   ship   ship

subway
지하철

[sʌ́bwéi 써브웨이]

subway   subway   subway

taxi
택시

[tǽksi 택씨]

taxi   taxi   taxi   taxi

train
기차

[trein 츄뢰인]

train   train   train   train

truck
트럭

[trʌk 츄럭]

truck   truck   truck   truck

1. 알파벳을 오른쪽 단어에 맞게 배열하고 따라 써봅시다.

❶ a, c, r — — — — — — — c — — — — — — — 자동차

❷ p, s, h, i — — — — — s — — — — — 배

❸ a, t, i ,x — — — — t — — — — 택시

❹ n,a,r,i,t — — — t — — — 기차

2. 영어에 맞은 우리말을 찾아 ○표를 해 봅시다.

| This is a taxi. | 저것은 택시이다. |
| | 이것은 택시이다. |

| That is a train. | 저것은기차이다. |
| | 저것은 트럭이다. |

| This is a car, | 저것은 자동차이다. |
| | 이것은 자동차이다. |

3. 알맞은 단어를 보기에서 찾아 빈칸에 써 넣고 아래 따라 써봅시다.

보기   This   That

❶ ⬚⬚⬚ is a car.

이것은 자동차이다.

is a car.

❷ ⬚⬚⬚ is a ship.

저것은 배이다.

is a ship.

❸ ⬚⬚⬚ is a bus.

저것은 버스이다.

is a bus.

27

3. 학교생활(1)

 단어를 배워 봅시다.

a desk

a teacher

a notebook

 문장을 배워 봅시다.

Stand up.

Sit down.

단어를 따라 써봅시다.

desk
책상 · 데스크

desk

desk

teacher
선생 · 티춰

teacher

teacher

notebook
공책 노우트북

notebook

notebook

문장을 따라 써봅시다.

Stand up.　　　Stand up.

Sit down.　　　Sit down.

Stand up.　　　Sit down.

단어를 배워 봅시다.

a bag

a chair

a lesson

 문장을 배워 봅시다.

30

⭐ 단어를 따라 써봅시다.

bag

가방 · 백

bag

bag

chair

의자 · 췌어

chair

chair

lesson

수업 · 레쓴

lesson

lesson

⭐ 문장을 따라 써봅시다.

This is a chair.   This is a chair.

This is a chair.   That is a window.

That is a window. That is a window.

This is a notebook.
이것은 공책이다.

That is a desk.
저것은 책상이다.

That is a chair.
저것은 의자이다.

문장을 따라 써봅시다.

This is a notebook.

This is a notebook.

That is a desk.

That is a desk.   That is a desk.

That is a chair.

That is a chair.   That is a chair.

album
앨범, 사진첩

[ǽlbəm 앨범]

album   album   album

bag
가방, 봉지

[bæg 백]

bag   bag   bag   bag

board
판자, 게시판

[bɔːrd 보-ㄹ드]

board   board   board

book
책

[buk 북]

book   book   book

class
수업, 학급

[klæs 클래스]

class   class   class

desk

책상

[desk 데스크]

desk   desk   desk

eraser

지우개

[iréisə́yér
이뢰이줘ㄹ]

eraser   eraser   eraser

learn

배우다

[lə́ːɾn 러–ㄹ언]

learn   learn   learn

lesson

수업

[lésn 렛쓴]

lesson   lesson   lesson

pen

펜

[pen 펜]

pen   pen   pen   pen   pen

pencil

연필

[pénsəl 펜쓸]

pencil   pencil   pencil

1. 알파벳을 오른쪽 단어에 맞게 배열하고 따라 써봅시다.

❶ s, c, l, s, a _____ 학급
___c___

❷ o, k, o, b _____ 책
___b___

❸ e, l, o, s, s, n _____ 수업
___l___

❹ e, c, l, n, p, i _____ 연필
___p___

2. 영어에 맞은 우리말을 찾아 ○표를 해 봅시다.

This is a bag.

저것은 상자이다.

이것은 가방이다.

That is a notebook.

저것은공책이다.

저것은 책이다.

This is a chair.

이것은 의자이다.

이것은 책상이다.

3. 알맞은 단어를 보기에서 찾아 빈칸에 써 넣고 아래 따라 써봅시다.

보기   down   This   up   That

❶ Stand _____.

일어서요.

Stand

❷ Sit _____.

앉아요.

Sit

❸ _____ is a desk.

저것은 책상이다.

is a desk.

단어를 배워 봅시다.

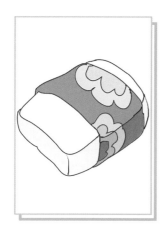

an eraser

an ink

a table

 문장을 배워 봅시다.

단어를 따라 써봅시다.

eraser

지우개 · 이레이져

eraser

eraser

ink

잉크 · 잉크

ink

ink

table

테이블 · 테이불

table

table

문장을 따라 써봅시다.

Come in.　　　Come in.

Come in.　　　Hello, Sung Won.

Hello, Sung Won.

단어를 배워 봅시다.

a crayon

teach

a pen

 문장을 배워 봅시다.

Give me a book.

Here you are.

⭐ 단어를 따라 써봅시다.

crayon

크레용 · 케이언

crayon

crayon

teach

가르치다 · 티취

teach

teach

pen

펜 · 펜

pen

pen

⭐ 문장을 따라 써봅시다.

Give me a book.

Here you are.　　Here you are.

Give me a book.　Here you are.

41

This is a crayon.
이것은 크레용이다.

That is a pen.
저것은 펜이다.

He teaches English.
그는 영어를 가르친다.

문장을 따라 써봅시다.

This is a crayon.

This is a crayon.   This is a crayon.

That is a pen.

That is a pen.   That is a pen.

He teaches English.

He teaches English.

pin
핀

[pin 핀]

pin   pin   pin   pin

school
학교, 수업

[skuːl 스꾸-울]

school   school   school

student
학생

[stjúːdənt
스츄-던트]

student   student   student

study
공부하다

[stʌ́di 스떠디]

study   study   study

table
테이블

[téibl 테이블]

table   table   table

teach
가르치다

[tiːtʃ 티-취]

teach   teach   teach

test
시험, 검사

[test 테스트]

test   test   test   test

camp
캠프

[kæmp 캠프]

camp   camp   camp

chalk
분필

[tʃɔːk 초어크]

chalk   chalk   chalk

computer
컴퓨터

[kəmpjúːtər 컴퓨-러ㄹ]

computer   computer   computer

crayon
크레용

[kréiən 크래이언]

crayon   crayon   crayon

1. 영어 단어를 우리말에 맞게 써 넣으세요.

❶ table

t

❷ eraser

e

❸ ink

i

❹ teach

t

2. 영어에 맞은 우리말을 찾아 ○표를 해 봅시다.

He teaches English.

그녀는 영어를 가르치고 있다.

그는 영어를 가르치고 있다.

That is a crayon.

저것은 크레용이다.

이것은 크레용이다.

This is a pen.

이것은 펜이다.

이것은 연필이다.

3. 알맞은 단어를 보기에서 찾아 빈칸에 써 넣고 아래 따라 써봅시다.

보기   Here   in   up   give

❶ Come _____.

들어와요.

_____

Come

❷ _____ me a book.

책을 줘요.

_____

me a book.

❸ _____ you are.

여기 있어요.

_____

you are.

5. 나의 이름

 단어를 배워 봅시다.

name

I

you

 문장을 배워 봅시다.

My name is Tom.

I am Sung Won.

48

단어를 따라 써봅시다.

name　　　I　　　you

| 이름 · 네임 | 나는 · 아이 | 너 · 유- |

name　　　I　　　you

name　　　I　　　you

문장을 따라 써봅시다.

My name is Tom.　My name is Tom.

I am Sung Won.　I am Sung Won.

단어를 배워 봅시다.

he

she

we

 문장을 배워 봅시다.

what is your name?

My name is Tom.

he

그가 · 히

he

he

she

그녀가 · 쉬

she

she

we

우리 · 위

we

we

⭐ 문장을 따라 써봅시다.

He is a boy.   He is a boy.

She is a girl.   She is a girl.

He is a boy.   She is a girl.

what is your name?
너의 이름은 무엇이니?

My name is Tom.
내 이름은 톰이야.

My name is Nancy.
내 이름은 낸시야.

문장을 따라 써봅시다.

What is your name?

What is your name?

What is your name?

My name is Tom.

My name is Tom.

My name is Tom.

My name is Nancy.

My name is Nancy.

My name is Nancy.

I
나는, 내가
[ai 아이]

I I I I I I I I

my
나의
[mɑí 마이]

my my my my my

you
너, 당신
[juː 유–]

you you you you

body
몸, 신체
[bɑ́di 바디]

body body body body

face
얼굴
[feis 페이스]

face face face face

hair
머리카락, 털

[hɛər 헤얼]

hair hair hair hair

head
머리

[hed 헤드]

head head head head

hand
손

[hænd 핸드]

hand hand hand hand

lip
입술

[lip 립]

lip lip lip lip lip lip

mouth
입

[mauθ 마웃쓰]

mouth mouth mouth

nose
코

[nouz 노우즈]

nose nose nose

1. 영어 단어를 우리말에 맞게 써 넣으세요.

❶ you

y

❷ he

h

❸ I

I

❹ she

s

2. 영어에 맞은 우리말을 찾아 ○표를 해 봅시다.

What is your name?

너의 이름은 무엇이니?

그의 이름은 무엇이니?

I am Nancy.

나는 낸시야.

그는 낸시야.

Goodbye Nance.

잘있어 낸시.

잘 가 낸시.

3. 알맞은 단어를 보기에서 찾아 빈칸에 써 넣고 아래 따라 써봅시다.

보기   what is   I am   My name

❶ _____ Sung Won.

나는 성원이야.

Sung Won.

❷ _____ your name?

너의 이름은 무엇이니?

your name?

❸ _____ is Tom.

나의 이름은 톰이야.

is Tom.

6. 가족

 단어를 배워 봅시다.

a family

a mother

a baby

 문장을 배워봅시다.

Who is he?

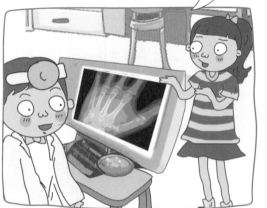

He is my father.

family

가족 · 훼밀리

family

family

mother

어머니 · 마덜

mother

mother

baby

아기 · 베이비

baby

baby

★ 문장을 따라써봅시다.

Who is he?   Who is he?

He is my father.   He is my father.

Who is he?   He is my father.

단어를 배워 봅시다.

a brother

a sister

an aunt

 문장을 배워 봅시다.

Who is she?

she is my mother.

brother
형제 · 브라덜

brother

brother

sister
여자형제 · 씨스털

sister

sister

aunt
아주머니 · 앤트

aunt

aunt

★ 문장을 따라 써 봅시다.

Who is she?   Who is she?

she is my mother. she is my mother.

Who is she?   she is my mother.

She is my sister.
그녀는 나의 누이야.

He is my brother.
그는 나의 형이야.

She is my mom.
그녀는 나의 엄마야.

문장을 따라 써 봅시다.

She is my sistere.

She is my sister.   She is my sister.
She is my sister.   She is my sister.

He is my brother.

He is my brother. He is my brother.
He is my brother. He is my brother.

She is my mom.

She is my mom.   She is my mom.
She is my mom.   She is my mom.

가족

brother
형제
[brʌðr 브롸덜]

brother　　brother　　brother

family
가족
[fǽməli 페믈리]

family　　family　　family

father
아버지
[fɑ́:ðər 퐈-덜]

fathe　　fathe　　fathe

dad/daddy
아빠
[dæd 대드]

dad/daddy　　dad/daddy

daughter
딸
[dɔ́:tər 더-러]

daughter　　daughter

64

grandmother	grandmothe	grandmothe
할머니		
[grǽndmʌ́:ðər 그랜드머더]		

mom	mom	mom	mom
엄마			
[mam 맘]			

mother	mother	mother	mother
어머니			
[mʌ́ðər 머덜]			

sister	sister	sister	sister	sister
여자형제, 언니				
[sístər 씨스털]				

son	son	son	son	son	son
아들					
[sɔn 썬]					

uncle	uncle	uncle	uncle	uncle
아저씨, 삼촌				
[ʌ́ŋkl 엉끌]				

1. 영어 단어를 우리말에 맞게 써 넣으세요.

❶ brother　　　　　　　　b

❷ mother　　　　　　　　m

❸ baby　　　　　　　　b

❹ family　　　　　　　　f

2. 영어에 맞은 우리말을 찾아 ○표를 해 봅시다.

| Who is he? | 그는 누구이니? |
| | 그녀는 누구이니? |

| He is my fatrer. | 그는 나의 아버지야. |
| | 그는 나의 삼촌이야. |

| She is my mother. | 그는 나의 어머니야. |
| | 그녀는 나의 어머니야. |

3. 알맞은 단어를 보기에서 찾아 빈칸에 써 넣고 아래 따라 써봅시다.

보기 She is   he is

❶ _____ my sister.

그녀는 나의 누나야.

_____

my sister.

❷ _____ my brother.

그는 나의 형이야.

_____

my brother.

❸ _____ my mom.

그녀는 나의 엄마야.

_____

my mom.

단어를 배워 봅시다.

 black

blue

color

 문장을 배워 봅시다.

What color is the truck?

It is black.

단어를 따라 써봅시다.

black

검은 · 블랙

black

black

blue

블루- · 파란

blue

blue

color

색깔 · 컬러-ㄹ

color

color

 문장을 따라 써봅시다.

What color is the truck?

It is black.   It is black.

What color is the truck?

단어를 배워 봅시다.

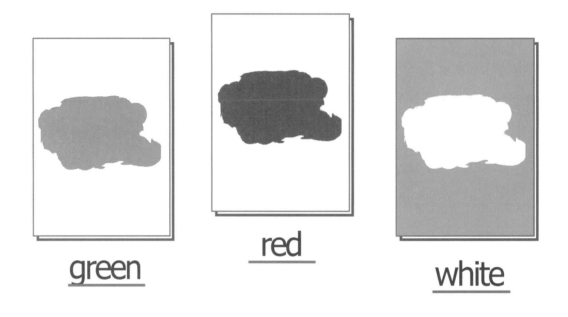

green

red

white

 문장을 배워 봅시다.

What color is the bus?

It is green.

⭐ 단어를 따라 써봅시다.

green	red	white
초록색 · 그뤼인	빨간색 · 레드	흰색 · 화이트

green   red   white

green   red   white

⭐ 문장을 따라 써봅시다.

What color is the bus?

It is green.   It is green.

What color is the bus?

What color is it?
그것은 무슨 색이니?

It is orange.
그것은 오랜지색이야.

It is blue.
그것은 파란색이야.

72

문장을 따라 써봅시다.

What color is it?

What color is it?   What color is it?

What color is it?   What color is it?

It is orange.

It is orange.   It is orange.

It is orange.   It is orange.

It is blue.

It is blue.   It is blue.

It is blue.   It is blue.

색

black
검은 색
[blæk 블랙]

black　black　black　black

blue
파란색
[bluː 블루-]

blue　blue　blue　blue

brown
갈색, 갈색의
[braun 브롸운]

brown　brown　brown

color
색깔
[kʌlər 컬러ㄹ]

color　color　color　color

gray
회색, 회색의
[grei 그뢰이]

gray　gray　gray　gray

orange
오렌지 색

[ɔ́ːrindʒ 오륀쥐]

orange   orange   orange

pink
분홍

[piŋk 핑크]

pink   pink   pink   pink

red
빨간색, 붉은

[red 뤠드]

red red red red red

silver
은, 은빛, 은의

[sílvər 씰붜얼]

silver silver silver silver

white
흰, 흰빛

[hwait 와이트]

white white white white

yellow
노랑

[jélou 옐로-]

yellow yellow yellow yellow

1. 영어 단어를 우리말에 맞게 써 넣으세요.

❶ red

r

❷ green

g

❸ color

c

❹ brown

b

2. 영어에 맞은 우리말을 찾아 ○표를 해 봅시다.

What color is the bag.

그 공은 무슨 색이니?

그 가방은 무슨 색이니?

It is brown.

그 것은 오랜지색이야.

그 것은 갈색이야.

It is blue.

그 것은 검은색이야.

그 것은 파란색이야.

3. 알맞은 단어를 보기에서 찾아 빈칸에 써 넣고 아래 따라 써봅시다.

보기   What color is   It is   blue

❶ _____ **the truck?**

그 트럭은 무슨 색이니?.

the truck?

❷ _____ **black.**

그것은 검은 색이야.

black.

❸ It is _____

그것은 파란색이야.

It is

8. 자연

 단어를 배워 봅시다.

moon

earth

grass

 문장을 배워 봅시다.

What is that?

It is grass.

단어를 따라 써봅시다.

moon

달 무-ㄴ

moon

moon

earth

지구 · 어-ㄹ쓰

earth

earth

grass

잔디 · 그뢰스

grass

grass

문장을 따라 써봅시다.

What is that?　　What is that?

It is grass.　　It is grass.

What is that?　　It is grass.

sun

sea

wind

★ 문장을 배워 봅시다.

What is that?

It is sun.

단어를 따라 써봅시다.

sun

태양 · 썬

sun

sun

sea

바다 · 씨-

sea

sea

wind

바람 · 윈드

wind

wind

문장을 따라 써봅시다.

What is that?　　What is that?

It is sun.　　It is sun.

What is that?　　It is sun.

What is that?
저것은 무엇이니?

It is the Sun.
그것은 해님이야.

It is the rainbow.
그것은 무지개야.

82

문장을 따라 써봅시다.

What is that?

What is that?　　　What is that?

What is that?　　　What is that?

It is the Sun.

It is the Sun.　　　It is the Sun.

It is the Sun.　　　It is the Sun.

It is the rainbow.

It is the rainbow.　It is the rainbow.

It is the rainbow.　It is the rainbow.

air
공기

[ɛər 에어ㄹ]

air　air　air　air　air　air

beach
물가, 바닷가

[biːtʃ비-잇취]

beach　beach　beach　beach

cloud
구름

[klaud클라우드]

cloud　cloud　cloud　cloud

earth
지구, 땅

[əːrθ어-ㄹ쓰]

earth　earth　earth　earth

field
들판

[fiːld쀠-ㄹ드]

field　field　field　field

grass
풀

[græs 그뢰쓰]

grass   grass   grass

island
섬

[áilənd 아일런드]

island   island   island

lake
호수

[leik 레익]

lake lake lake lake lake lake

moon
달

[muːn 무-ㄴ]

moon   moon   moon

mountain
산

[mauntən 마운튼]

mountain   mountain   mountain

rainbow
무지개

[réinbóu 뢰인보우]

rainbow   rainbow   rainbow

1. 영어 단어를 우리말에 맞게 써 넣으세요.

❶ moon   r

❷ wind   g

❸ grass   c

❹ sun   b

2. 서로 맞은 것끼리 선으로 연결해 봅시다.

What is that?	그것은 무지게야.
It is the sun.	저것은 무엇이니?
It is the rainbow.	그것은 해님이야.

3. 알맞은 단어를 보기에서 찾아 빈칸에 써 넣고 아래 따라 써봅시다.

보기   **What is**   **It is**

❶ ⬜⬜⬜⬜ sun.

그것은 해님이야.

sun.

❷ ⬜⬜⬜⬜ that?

저것은 무엇이니?

that.

❸ ⬜⬜⬜ grass.

그것은 잔디야.

grass.

9. 과일 .음식

 단어를 배워 봅시다.

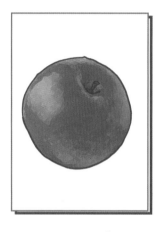

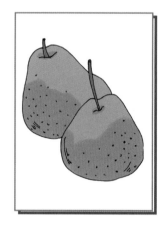

an apple

a grape

a pear

 문장을 배워 봅시다.

⭐ 단어를 따라 써봅시다.

apple
사과 · 애플

apple

apple

grape
포도 · 그레이프

grape

grape

pear
배 · 페얼

pear

pear

⭐ 문장을 따라 써봅시다.

Do you like apples?

Yes, I do.   Yes, I do.

Do you like apples?

단어를 배워 봅시다.

an egg

food

 문장을 배워 봅시다.

90

단어를 따라 써봅시다.

butter

벼터 · 버터

butter

butter

egg

달걀 · 에그

egg

egg

food

음식 · 푸드

food

food

⭐ 문장을 따라 써봅시다.

What do you like?

I like pizza.   I like pizza.

What do you like?

What do you like?
넌 무엇을 좋아하니?

I like cake.
나는 케익을 좋아해.

I like a tomato.
나는 토마토를 좋아해.

문장을 따라 써봅시다.

What do you like?

What do you like?

What do you like?

I like cake.

I like cake.   I like cake.

I like cake.   I like cake.

I like a tomato.

I like a tomato.   I like a tomato.

I like a tomato.   I like a tomato.

apple
사과

[ǽpəl 애쁠]

apple apple apple

banana
바나나

[bənǽnə
버내너]

banana banana banana

corn
옥수수

[kɔːrn 콘]

corn corn corn

grape
포도

[greip 그뢰입]

grape grape grape

tomato
토마토

[təméitou
터메이토]

tomato tomato tomato

butter
버터

[bʌ́tər 버러ㄹ]

butte   butte   butte

bread
빵

[bred 브레드]

bread   bread   bread

cake
케이크

[keik 케이크]

cake   cake   cake

cheese
치즈

[tʃiːz 취-즈]

cheese   cheese   cheese

cream
크림

[kriːm크뤼-임]

cream   cream   cream

candy
사탕

[kǽndi 캔디]

candy   candy   candy

1. 영어 단어를 우리말에 맞게 써 넣으세요.

❶ butter

b

❷ grape

g

❸ pear

p

❹ food

f

2. 서로 맞은 것끼리 선으로 연결해 봅시다.

What do you like?

나는 케익을 좋아해.

I like cake.

나는 토마토를 좋아해.

I like a tomato.

너는 무엇을 좋아하니?

3. 알맞은 단어를 보기에서 찾아 빈칸에 써 넣고 아래 따라 써봅시다.

보기　Do you　　I like　　What do

❶ [_____] you like?

너는 무엇을 좋아하니?

you like?

❷ [_____] like apples?

너는 사과를 좋아하니?

like apples?

❸ [_____] bread.

나는 빵을 좋아해.

bread.

10. 동식물

 단어를 배워 봅시다.

an ant

a tiger

a monkey

 문장을 배워 봅시다.

Do you have a monkey?

No, I don't.

단어를 따라 써봅시다.

ant

개미 · 앤트

ant

ant

tiger

호랑이 · 타이거

tiger

tiger

monkey

원숭이 · 멍키

monkey

monkey

문장을 따라 써봅시다.

Do you have a monkey?

No, I don't.   No, I don't.

Do you have a monkey?

a flower

a rose

a tulip

문장을 배워 봅시다.

What is this flower?

It is a tulip.

단어를 따라 써봅시다.

flower

꽃 · 플라우어

flower

flower

rose

장미 · 로즈

rose

rose

tulip

튤립 · 튜립

tulip

tulip

문장을 따라 써봅시다.

What is this flower?

It is a tulip.   It is a tulip.

What is this flower?

Do you have a puppy?
너는 강아지를 가지고 있니?

No, I don't.
아니, 난 없어.

I have a rabbit.
나는 토끼를 가지고 있어.

문장을 따라 써봅시다.

Do you have a puppy?

Do you have a puppy?

No, I don't.

No, I don't.   No, I don't.

I have a rabbit.

I have a rabbit.   I have a rabbit.

animal
동물, 짐승

[ǽnəməl 애니멀]

animal   animal   animal

ant
개미

[ænt 앤트]

ant   ant   ant   ant   ant

bear
곰

[bɛər 베어-ㄹ]

bear   bear   bear   bear

bird
새

[bəːrd 버얼드]

bird   bird   bird   bird

cat
고양이

[kæt 캣]

cat   cat   cat   cat   cat

chicken

닭

[tʃíkən 취킨]

chicken   chicken   chicken

dog

개

[dɔːg 더-ㄱ]

dog   dog   dog   dog

duck

오리

[dʌk 덕]

duck   duck   duck   duck

lion

사자

[láiən 라이언]

lion lion lion lion lion lion

monkey

원숭이

[mʌ́ŋki 멍끼]

monke   monke   monke

tiger

호랑이

[táigər 타이걸]

tiger   tiger   tiger   tiger

1. 영어 단어를 우리말에 맞게 써 넣으세요.

① tiger

t

② monkey

m

③ ant

a

④ flower

f

2. 서로 맞은 것끼리 선으로 연결해 봅시다.

Do you have a monkey?

너는 호랑이를 가지고 있니?

What is this flower?

이것은 무슨 꽃이니?

Do you have a tiger?

너는 원숭이를 가지고 있니?

3. 알맞은 단어를 보기에서 찾아 빈칸에 써 넣고 아래 따라 써봅시다.

보기   Do you have   I have

❶ _____ a monkey?

너는 원숭이를 가지고 있니?

_____

a monkey?

❷ _____ a puppy?

너는 강아지를 가지고 있니?

_____

a puppy?

❸ _____ a rabbit.

나는 토끼를 가지고 있어.

_____

a rabbit.

단어를 배워 봅시다.

a doctor

a cook

a teacher

 문장을 배워 봅시다.

단어를 따라 써봅시다.

doctor

| 의사 · 닥터 |

doctor

doctor

cook

| 요리사 · 쿡 |

cook

cook

teacher

| 선생 · 티춰 |

teacher

teacher

⭐ 문장을 따라 써봅시다.

What is his job?　What is his job?

He is a doctor.　He is a doctor.

What is his job?　He is a doctor.

단어를 배워 봅시다.

a nurse

a driver

a mailman

 문장을 배워봅시다.

What is her job?

She is a nurse.

단어를 따라 써봅시다.

nurse

간호사 · 널쓰

nurse

nurse

driver

운전시 · 드라이버

driver

driver

mailman

우편집배원 · 메일맨

mailman

mailman

문장을 따라써봅시다.

What is her job?　What is her job?

She is a nurse.　She is a nurse.

What is her job?　She is a nurse.

What is his job?
그의 직업은 무엇이니?

He is a farmer.
그는 농부야.

He is a mailman.
그는 우편배달부야.

문장을 따라 써 봅시다.

What is his job?

What is his job?

What is his job?

He is a farmer.

He is a farmer.

He is a farmer.

He is a mailman.

He is a mailman.

He is a mailman.

captain
선장, 우두머리

[kǽptin 캡틴]

captain   captain   captain

cook
요리사

[kúk 쿡]

cook   cook   cook

doctor
의사

[dάktər닥터ㄹ]

doctor   doctor   doctor

farmer
농부

[kúk 파-머-]

farmer   farmer   farmer

job
일, 직업

[dʒab 좝]

job   job   job   job   job

nurse
간호사

[nəːrs 널쓰]

nurse   nurse   nurse

pilot
조종사

[páilət 파일럿]

pilot   pilot   pilot   pilot

police
경찰

[pəlíːs 펄리-스]

police   police   police

scientist
과학자

[saiəntist
사이언티스트]

scientist   scientist   scientist

soldier
군인

[souldʒə(r)
소울저]

soldier   soldier   soldier

talent
탤런트

[tælənt 탤런트]

talent   talent   talent

1. 영어 단어를 우리말에 맞게 써 넣으세요.

❶ cook

c _____

❷ doctor

d _____

❸ nurse

n _____

❹ driver

d _____

2. 서로 맞은 것끼리 선으로 연결해 봅시다.

He is a farmer.	그의 직업이 무엇이니?
What is his job?	그는 요리사야.
He is a cook.	그는 농부야.

3. 알맞은 단어를 보기에서 찾아 빈칸에 써 넣고 아래 따라 써봅시다.

보기 What is   He is   She is

❶ _____ a nurse.

그녀는 간호사야.

a nurse.

❷ _____ his job?

그의 직업은 무엇이니?

his job?

❸ _____ a doctor.

그는 의사야.

a doctor.

12. 우리 집

 단어를 배워 봅시다.

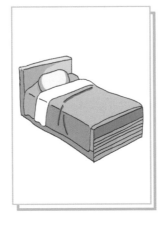

a home

a bed

a kitchen

 문장을 배워 봅시다.

Where is she?

She is in the kichen.

단어를 따라써 봅시다.

home

집 · 홈

home

home

bed

침대 · 뱃

bed

bed

kitchen

부엌 · 킷췬

kitchen

kitchen

문장을 따라써봅시다.

Where is she?　　Where is she?

She is in the kichen.

She is in the kichen.

단어를 배워봅시다.

 a curtain

a door

a key

 문장을 배워봅시다.

120

단어를 따라써 봅시다.

curtain

커튼 · 커튼

curtain

curtain

door

문 · 도얼

door

door

key

열쇠 · 키-

key

key

문장을 따라써봅시다.

What is he doing now?

He is sleeping.   He is sleeping.

What is he doing now?

What is she doing?
그녀는 무엇을 하고 있나요?

She is cooking.
그녀는 요리를 하고 있어요.

He is studying English.
그는 영어 공부를 하고 있어요.

문장을 따라 써 봅시다.

What is she doing?

What is she doing?

What is she doing?

She is cooking.

She is cooking.

She is cooking.

He is studying English.

He is studying English.

He is studying English.

우리집

apartment
아파트

[əpáːrtmənt
아파-알트먼트]

apartment   apartment

bed
침대

[bed 뱃]

bed   bed   bed   bed

bench
긴 의자, 벤치

[bentʃ 벤취]

bench   bench   bench

curtain
커튼

[kə́ːrtn 커튼]

curtain   curtain   curtain

door
문

[dɔːr 도얼]

door   door   door   door

garden

정원

[gáːrdn 가-든]

garden   garden   garden

home

집

[hóum 홈]

home   home   home

house

집

[haus 하우스]

house   house   house

kitchen

부엌

[kítʃin 킷췬]

kitchen   kitchen   kitchen

roof

지붕

[ruːf 루-프]

roof   roof   roof   roof

room

방

[ruːm 루-움]

room   room   room   room

1. 영어 단어를 우리말에 맞게 써 넣으세요.

❶ kitchen

k

❷ door

d

❸ bed

b

❹ home

h

2. 서로 맞은 것끼리 선으로 연결해 봅시다.

She is studying English.

그녀는 무엇을 하고 있니?

She is cooking.

그녀는 영어를 공부하고 있어.

What is she doing?

그녀는 요리를 하고 있어.

3. 알맞은 단어를 보기에서 찾아 빈칸에 써 넣고 아래 따라 써봅시다.

보기   She is   He is   Where

❶ _____ is she?

그녀는 어디에 있나요?

_____

is she?

❷ _____ in the kichen.

그녀는 부엌에 있어요.

_____

in the kichen.

❸ _____ sleeping.

그는 자고 있어요.

_____

sleeping.

🎒 해 답

p,16p

1.
① hello - 안녕

② goodbye-잘 있어

③ trank-고마워

④ you-너

3.
① hello - Sung-won

② goodbye- Nancy

③ trank-you

④ goodbye Sung-won

p,26p

1.
① car   ② ship
③ taxi   ④ train

2.
① this is a taxi.
   이것은 택시이다.
② that is a train.
   저것은 기차이다.
③ this is acar
   이것은 자동차이다.

3.
① this is a car.

② that is a ship.

③ that is a bus.

p,36p

1.
① class   ② book
③ lesson   ④ pencil

2.
① this is a bag.
   이것은 가방이다.
② that is a notebook.
   저것은 공책이다.
③ this is a chair.
   저것은 의자이다.

3.
① stand up.

② sit down

③ that is a desk.

p,46p

1.
① 책상   ② 지우개
③ 잉크   ④ 가르치다

2.

① He teaches English.

그는 영어를 가르치고 있다.

② that is a crayon.

저것은 크레용이다.

③ this is a pen.

이것은 펜이다.

3.

① com in.

②Give me a book.

③ Here you are.

p,56p

1.

① 너

② 그

③ 나

④ 그녀

2.

① What is your name?

너의 이름은 무엇이니?

② I am Nancy.

나는 낸시야.

③ Goodbye Nancy.

잘있어 낸시.

3.

① I am Sung won.

② What is your name?

③ My name is Tom.

p,66p

1.

① 남자 형제

② 어머니

③ 아기

④ 가족

2.

① What is he?

그는 누구이니?

② He is my fatrer.

그는 나의 아버지야.

③ She is my mother.

그녀는 나의 어머니야.

3.

① She is my sister.

② He is my brother.

③ She is my mom.

🎒 해 답

p,76p

1.
① 뻴간색   ② 녹색

③ 색깔   ④ 갈색

2.
① What color is the bag.
그 가방은 무슨 색이니?
② It is brown.
그것은 갈색이야.
③ It is blue.
그것은 파란 색이야.

3.
① What color is the truck?
② It is black.
③ It is blue.

p,86p

1.
① 달   ② 바람
③ 잔디   ④ 해

2.
① What is that?
저것은 무엇이니??

② It is the sun.
그것은 해님이야.
③ It is the rainbow.
그것은 무지게야.

3.
① It is sun.
② What is that?
③ It is grass.

p,96p

1.
① 버터   ② 포도
③ 배   ④ 음식

2.
① What do you like?
너는 무엇을 좋아하니?
② I like cake.
나는 케익을 좋아해.
③ I like a tomato.
나는 토마토를 좋아해.

3.
① What do you like?
② Do you like apples.
③ I like bread.

p,106p

1.

① 호랑이　② 원숭이

③ 개미　　④ 꽃

2.

① Do you have a monkey?
너는 원숭이 가지고 있니?

② What is this flower?
이것은 무슨 꽃이니?

③ Do you have a tige?
너는 호랑이 가지고 있니?

3.

① Do you have a monkey?

② Do you have a puppy?

③ I have a rabbit

p,116p

1.

① 요리사　② 의사

③ 간호사　④ 운전사

2.

① He is famer.
그는 농부야.

② What is his job?
그의 직업이 무엇이니?

③ He is a cook.
그는 요리사야.

3.

① She is a nurse.

② What is his job?

③ He is a doctor.

p,126p

1.

① 부엌

② 문

③ 침대

④ 집

2.

① She is studying English.
그녀는 영어공부를 하고 있어.

② She is cooking.
그녀는 요리를 하고 있어.

③ What is she doing?
그녀는 무엇을 하고 았니?

3.

① Where is she?

② She is in the kichen.

③ He is sleeping.

뉴-영어 교과서 따라쓰기
(문장 · 단어편)

초판 1쇄 발행 2016년 4월 20일

글 Y&M 어학 연구소

펴낸이 서영희 | **펴낸곳** 와이 앤 엠

편집 임명아 | **책임교정** 하연정

본문인쇄 명성 인쇄 | **제책** 정화 제책

제작 이윤식 | **마케팅** 강성태

주소 120-848 서울시 서대문구 홍은동 376-28

전화 (02)308-3891 | Fax (02)308-3892

E-mail yam3891@naver.com

등록 2007년 8월 29일 제312-2007-000040호

ISBN 978-89-93557-71-8 63740

본사는 출판물 윤리강령을 준수합니다.